IF YOU HAD TO CHOOSE,
What Would You Do?

IF YOU HAD TO CHOOSE,
What Would You Do?

Sandra McLeod Humphrey

Prometheus Books

59 John Glenn Drive
Amherst, New York 14228-2119

Published 1995 by Prometheus Books

Inquiries should be addressed to
Prometheus Books, 59 John Glenn Drive, Amherst, New York 14228–2197.
VOICE: 716–691–0133, ext. 207.
FAX: 716–564–2711.
WWW.PROMETHEUSBOOKS.COM

20 19 18 17 16   17 16 15 14 13

Interior design by Jacqueline Cooke
Illustrated by Brian Strassburg

Library of Congress Cataloging-in-Publication Data

Humphrey, Sandra McLeod.
   If you had to choose, what would you do? / Sandra McLeod Humphrey ; illustrated by Brian Strassburg.
        p.   cm.
   Summary: Presents a number of scenarios involving ethical dilemmas and asks the reader to decide what to do.
   ISBN-13: 978–1–57392-010-0 (pbk. : alk. paper)
   ISBN-10: 1–57392-010-X (pbk. : alk. paper)
   1. Ethics—Juvenile literature. 2. Children—Conduct of life. [1. Conduct of life. 2. Ethics.] I. Strassburg, Brian, ill. II. Title.
BJ1631.H85   1995
170—dc20   95–20056
                                                                                       CIP
                                                                                        AC

Printed in the United States of America on acid-free paper

Dedicated to young people everywhere
and to those who care about them.

Contents

A Note to Adults

It is never too soon to begin talking with our young people about personal values and helping them define their own code of moral conduct. The twenty-five problem situations presented in this book have been developed to help you talk to your children about values in as enjoyable and as natural a way as possible. I hope these discussions will help them develop a sense of direction and purpose to their lives resulting in more rewarding and more fulfilling experiences not only for them but also for those whose lives may be touched by their actions and choices.

The roles we play in society and the values we express have changed dramatically in recent years. As society's moral guidelines become increasingly more ambiguous, it is essential that we all have our basic code of ethics well crystallized in our own minds. We must guard against being unduly influenced by peer pressure in order to act according to our individual conscience and do what we know is right for us, even if sometimes it may mean standing alone.

As you read the twenty-five problem situations, you will note that there is certainly no one "correct" answer or solution to each problem, but rather there may be many possible solutions, depending on each individual's ingenuity and particular value system. More important than the "correct" solution is the *process* involved in making a choice or deciding upon a course of action.

The process provides the opportunity for you and your youngster to discuss the various alternatives under consideration. The discussion, once begun on a specific level, can then lead to broader issues. It is then relatively easy to make the transition to more general issues, which can facilitate meaningful dialogue. The important thing is to give your young person the opportunity to think about and talk about his/her values.

The sharing of ideas can be a pleasurable learning experience for all concerned as young people are given the opportunity to test some of their ideas in a safe setting. It is not so important that there is always mutual agreement regarding the proposed solutions but that there is the opportunity for youngsters to share their thoughts and feelings with someone they trust and in whose judgment they have confidence.

This book can serve as a comfortable vehicle for facilitating adult-child communication in general and discussions about moral, social, and ethical issues in particular. Parents and teachers should feel free to expand and personalize the dialogue as much as possible.

Sometimes you may want to ask your young person with which character he/she most strongly identifies and why. This can give you additional insight with respect to the child's perception of himself/herself in social situations, in athletic competitions, in the classroom, in relation to peer groups, in relation to other family members, and so on.

You may also find yourself making the natural transition from the specific problem situations in the book to a discussion of issues more pertinent to your particular circumstances. You may even want to create problem situations of your own.

Above all, use this book in any way that best facilitates meaningful communication between you and your youngster. Remember, it is just a starting point. The rest is up to you.

A Note to the Young Reader

Life will be a lot easier and also a lot more fun if you have strong beliefs and know what your values are. Sometimes different people may tell you different things, but if you know what you believe, then you will be able to do what is right regardless of what other people do or tell *you* to do.

The whole point of this book is to encourage you to think about what you would do in each of the twenty-five stories and why you would do it. There is often no one "right" answer. Just think about what you would do in that situation and then share your ideas with someone else. This can be a parent, a teacher, a friend—it can be anyone. Sharing your ideas with others can help you decide just what your values really are.

In some of the stories you may find yourself strongly attracted to one of the characters. It can then be fun to share with your parent or friend why you think you feel so close to that particular character. You may even want to ask the other person which character he or she feels most attracted to.

Now, last but most important: Have fun with this book! Talk over the stories with different people and sometimes just read them when you are by yourself if you feel like it. Whether alone or with others, enjoy this book the same way you would enjoy a good friend.

If You Had to Choose, What Would You Do?

All Systems Go!

Scott and Alan had looked forward all week to going to the neighborhood movie theater Saturday afternoon to see a scary horror film.

Finally it was Saturday. Scott's dad dropped them off in front of the theater and told them he'd be back to pick them up at the same spot after the movie.

While they waited for the ticket window to open, the boys wandered around to the back of the theater. There they saw a kid tossing plastic bags full of trash into the big blue dumpster.

The kid was wearing a purple Central High School sweatshirt and a blue baseball cap. Even from the back he looked a lot like Alan's older brother, Jake. Then the kid turned around and the boys saw that it *was* Jake.

Jake waved to them and gave the boys a "high-five." He jogged over to them flashing a big smile.

"Boy, are you guys in luck. I'm just cleaning out the theater before the one o'clock show, and no one else is in there yet. I can sneak both of you in before the ticket window even opens."

The boys couldn't believe it. They were going to get to see the movie *for free*. Sometimes it's really great having a big brother, Alan thought, especially one who worked at the movie theater.

If they didn't have to buy tickets for the movie, then they could use their money for video games at the mall. Boy, Jake was right. This really was their lucky day. It looked like it was "All systems go!"

Jake held the side door open for them, but Scott just wasn't sure he wanted to do it. He could hear his dad's voice telling him that he should do what he knew was right even if his friends did something else.

Scott shook his head. "I don't think I want to sneak in. I'll just pay for my ticket and then meet you inside."

Jake grinned. "You mean you're gonna pass up a chance like this? You're really weird, man. This theater makes megabucks and, believe me, it's not going to go broke just because you don't buy a ticket. Come on, Alan, you're not going to be a jerk, are you?"

Alan shook his head. "Not on your life. Let me in, bro. Oh, boy, wait till the guys at school hear about this. Little Scott was too chicken to sneak into a dumb movie. Come on, Scott, this is your last chance. I'm going in, with or without you."

Scott wasn't sure what he should do. He knew that sneaking into the movie wasn't right, but Jake had a point. They wouldn't really be hurting anyone else. It wasn't like the movie theater was going to go broke without his three bucks.

18

He was sure that just about any other guy in his class would sneak into the movie without even thinking twice about it. So why shouldn't he? Did he want the other guys at school to think he was a real jerk—someone who was chicken?

Whatever he was going to do, he had to do it now. Alan and Jake were holding the door open for him, waiting for him to make up his mind.

If you were Scott, and you had to choose, what would *you* do? Why?

More to think about:

Why do you think Jake offered to get the boys into the movie for free?

Do you think the other kids at Scott's school will think he's a real jerk if he doesn't sneak into the movie?

How do you decide whether something is wrong or right? Is it just a question of whether anyone else will get hurt?

Both Alan and Jake say that nobody will get hurt. Is that true?

Best Friends

Lisa and Betsy had been best friends since the first grade. Now they were in the fourth grade together at the Westwood Elementary School and they were still best friends.

It was the first week of school and Lisa and Betsy knew almost everyone in their class. The same kids were back from last year and there was only one new kid in their class.

The new kid was a girl named Trisha. At recess time Trisha usually played by herself on the tire swings, but today she came over to the jungle gym where Lisa and Betsy were playing and asked if she could play with them.

Betsy told Trisha that only two could play what they were playing and told her to go play with someone else. Trisha didn't say anything. She just stared down at her tennis shoes and then slowly walked back to the tire swings where she stayed by herself until the bell rang and everyone returned to Ms. Emerson's class.

On the way home later that day, Lisa and Betsy sat on the first seat of the school bus as usual. Trisha walked past them without looking at either one of them and sat somewhere behind them.

When Lisa got off the bus at her bus stop and waited for the bus to pull away from the curb, she noticed that Trisha was sitting in a seat all by herself.

By the time dinner was ready, Lisa was feeling pretty miserable. She pictured Trisha sitting on the school bus by herself, playing on the playground by herself, and eating lunch in the lunchroom by herself.

Lisa had never been alone like that because she had always had Betsy for a best friend. She knew that Betsy didn't want to play with Trisha, but then Betsy never wanted to play with anyone except Lisa. She always told Lisa that "special friends" had to stick together and not share their secrets with anyone else.

Maybe Lisa could try to talk Betsy into playing with Trisha, at least until Trisha had a chance to make some friends of her own. That didn't mean they had to share their secrets with her. But what if Betsy said NO?

Lisa wanted Trisha to feel welcome to her new school, but why should *she* get stuck with Trisha's problem? There were other kids in the class that Trisha could play with. Just because Betsy had said no didn't mean that all the other kids would say no, too. But after one kid refused to play with you, it was probably pretty hard to try again. What if the next kid said no, too?

Maybe Lisa could ask Ms. Emerson to help Trisha get a friend. But what if Ms. Emerson asked Lisa to be Trisha's friend until Trisha made some friends of her own? Then Lisa would be in the same mess she was in now—trying to help Trisha but also trying to keep Betsy as a friend.

22

What if Lisa just told Betsy that she was going to play with Trisha whether Betsy liked it or not? Would Betsy stop being her best friend? Then what? Lisa might have to make some new friends if Betsy didn't want to be her friend after that. But maybe Betsy would give in and agree to play with Trisha too, at least for a while.

Lisa knew that she could always ask her mom. Her mom probably had problems with friends when she was younger . . . a *lot* younger. Maybe her mom couldn't even remember that far back. But maybe she could help somehow.

Lisa knew one thing for sure: Trisha needed a friend and Lisa knew that she wanted to help her. She just didn't know what to do.

If you were Lisa, and you had to choose, what would *you* do? Why?

More to think about:

Why should Lisa even try to be friends with Trisha?

Couldn't Trisha just find other kids to play with?

Why do you think Betsy is so unwilling to play with Trisha?

Why doesn't Trisha say something to help make friends with Betsy and Lisa?

Do you think Ms. Emerson knows that Trisha is having trouble making friends?

The Blackboard Blues

"Who would like to feed the fish?" Ms. Sanders asked her first-grade class. Almost everyone raised their hands, and Becky was given the job for the month of September.

Mark felt angry, very angry. He had raised his hand, too. Why was Becky chosen and not him?

"Now who would like to be my special helper for the month of September and help pass out papers and sharpen pencils?"

Again, almost every hand shot up. This time Larry was chosen. By the time Ms. Sanders got to the last job on her list, most of the kids in the class had been given jobs.

"Now who would like to help me clean the blackboards and the erasers every day for the month of September?"

No hands went up. Mark didn't raise his hand either. If he couldn't feed the fish, he didn't want any job. Let some other kid clean the dumb blackboards and erasers.

25

That night at dinner Mark told his family about his day at school and how Becky had been given the job *he* wanted. He also told his family how he didn't volunteer for any of the other jobs after that.

"Way to go, bro," said his older brother Ben. "That'll show them. Why should you get stuck with a job no one else wants?"

Dad studied the spaghetti on his fork for a minute then laid his fork down on his plate. "Ben does have a point, Mark, but what if no one offers to help Ms. Sanders clean the blackboards? Then what happens?"

Mark shrugged and stabbed a meatball with his fork. "I guess then she'll be stuck cleaning them by herself. That's *her* problem."

Mom passed the spaghetti bowl to Mark and then helped herself to some more salad. "Whose turn is it to help with the dishes tonight? I cooked dinner, so I know it's not my turn to do the dishes."

Both boys stared at their plates. Finally Ben asked, "Does that mean that whoever does the dishes has to scrub out the spaghetti pot, too?"

"You got it," his mom replied, smiling. "This family is a team. We all work together to help each other. Do you think it would be fair if I did all the cooking and all the dishes every day? Or if I got stuck with all the jobs no one else wanted?"

The boys looked at each other. "But we've got school and piano lessons and soccer practice," Ben responded. "We're really busy."

Mom smiled again. "And I've got my job plus this house to take care of plus the grocery shopping and the meals to plan. So I guess I'm just about as busy as you boys. I'm sure glad I have both of you to help me. I'd be worn out in no time if I had to do everything myself."

26

Dad nodded in agreement. "And that's why I help your mother with some of the indoor work and she helps me with some of the yard work. It wouldn't be much fun if one person got stuck with everything. When we work as a team and everyone does his share, then no one person gets stuck with more than he can handle."

Ben shrugged. "Okay, I get the picture. I guess that means it's my turn to get stuck with the spaghetti pot. Again."

Dad then looked at Mark. "And what about Ms. Sanders? Do you think anyone is going to volunteer tomorrow to help her clean the blackboards or do you think everyone's going to wait for someone else to volunteer?"

If you were Mark, and you had to choose, what would *you* do? Why?

More to think about:

Who do you think should feed the fish, pass out the papers, sharpen the pencils, and clean the blackboards? Do you think Ms. Sanders should do these jobs?

Why doesn't Mark want to clean the blackboards?

Do you think his brother gave him good advice?

If Mark and his classmates help Ms. Sanders with the jobs, do you think they will feel more that the class is really theirs and that they are all important members of a "team"?

Color Me Different

Having an older brother could sometimes be a real bummer, Doug told himself again for the zillionth time.

Doug slammed his school books down on the kitchen counter and helped himself to some leftover meat loaf and a glass of milk while he thought about his brother.

Gene was five years older and already in junior high. To hear everybody talk, Gene was just about perfect. Gene could shoot baskets like Michael Jordan. He could swim like a fish. And now Gene had made the track team his first year in junior high. Gene got straight As in everything, and he even kept his room clean.

Everywhere Doug went, it was the same story. Everyone compared him to Gene. Gene did this and Gene did that. He was tired of hearing about Gene.

Even Gene's charcoal sketches were still hanging in the student art center at Doug's school. Doug didn't have an artistic bone in his body, and he never would have unless someone gave him a major transplant.

Gene's was a tough act—an impossible act—to follow. And sometimes Doug wished he didn't have a brother at all, especially an older brother.

But one day Doug finally had a chance to even things up a little. For once in his life Gene might just end up looking dumb. And it would be so easy.

You see, Gene's art folder was all ready to present to his class the next day. It was his turn to show his art class the animal sketches he had made at the zoo two weeks earlier. Gene was really proud of his work and had spent the last few days making a special folder for his sketches.

Phil, one of the guys in Gene's class, told Doug that it would be a great joke to switch a few pictures while Gene was at soccer practice.

Doug worked on his math until Gene left for his soccer practice. Then he opened the art folder. There must have been at least fifteen sketches there. Doug had to admit, they looked pretty good, even to him.

Doug pictured how it would be the next day when Gene stood up in front of his whole class and opened his art folder. Instead of his animal sketches, there would be nothing but blank paper.

No real harm would be done. Mr. James, the art teacher, would just tell Gene to bring the right material the next day. But boy would Gene be embarrassed. Doug wished he could be there to see his brother's face.

Doug knew that Gene would never do anything like that to him. But, after all, it was just a joke. Maybe it would be good for Gene to feel a little dumb for once in his life.

Doug removed Gene's sketches from the pocket of the folder and slipped in the blank sheets in their place. But he didn't feel like laughing. He didn't feel good at all.

There was still time to slip the sketches back into the folder and forget the whole thing. But then he would have to explain to Phil why he chickened out.

Doug heard his dad calling him for dinner. He knew he had to make up his mind. Should he leave the blank paper in the folder or should he put Gene's sketches back?

If you were Doug, and you had to choose, what would *you* do? Why?

More to think about:

Why do you think Phil wants Doug to switch Gene's art papers?

How do you think Gene would feel if he started to give his talk to his class and then discovered he didn't have his sketches?

Do you think switching the art papers would just be a big joke?

How do you think Doug would feel if someone played this kind of joke on him?

Declaration of War

Dan crumpled up his math paper and threw it in the trash. Then he began again. It seemed he was spending half his life just doing homework.

Life in the fourth grade had become one big disaster with the arrival of Mrs. Henderson, the new teaching assistant. Mrs. Henderson never smiled, never joked with the kids, and she insisted on being called *Mrs.* Henderson. She was very strict when checking their homework papers. She took off points for words that weren't spelled exactly right and she even took off points if you forgot to put a period at the end of a sentence.

The kids in Dan's class called her "Mrs. Grizzly" behind her back. Dan had to admit that sometimes she looked like a very big, very grumpy brown bear.

Some of the kids thought Mrs. Henderson must be at least eighty years old, but Dan thought fifty was more like it. He knew she hadn't taught school for more than twenty years, because she didn't even know anything about computers.

After her husband died, Mrs. Henderson had to find a job, and since she hadn't taught for such a long time, she could only be a teaching assistant. Dan's class somehow got stuck with her. She wasn't happy. The kids weren't happy. No one was happy.

Now Mrs. Henderson was threatening to take points off for neatness if your homework paper was the least little bit messy. Things were going from bad to worse fast.

Dan found himself facing a big problem when only a week before Valentine's Day his whole class decided to declare war on Mrs. Henderson. The class had voted to buy their regular teacher, Ms. Emerson, a big box of chocolates. Then they voted not to buy Mrs. Henderson anything, not even a card.

Dan tried to try to talk his classmates into buying a card, at least. He even offered to pay for it himself, but they voted again and the answer was no.

Dan knew that if he bought Mrs. Henderson something after the class had voted not to, he would be in big trouble with all his friends. After all, the class had declared war on Mrs. Henderson and that would make Dan a traitor.

He had a feeling this was quickly turning into one of those "no-win" situations he was always hearing about. Either he was going to have the whole class mad at him if he bought Mrs. Henderson a card or he was going to be mad at himself if he didn't do what he thought was right.

It was really Mrs. Henderson's fault. If she wasn't such a bear, he wouldn't even have this problem.

Maybe Dan could get his mom to talk to Mrs. Henderson and tell her to "lighten up." Not likely. Mom actually *liked* what Mrs. Henderson was doing. She told him that learning good work habits now was going to prepare him for life later on.

Wrong! The only thing Mrs. Henderson was preparing him for was the Marines. She would have made a great drill sergeant.

What about talking to Mrs. Henderson himself and telling her how the kids felt? He felt his stomach turn upside down at that thought. No way was he going to face her all by himself.

What if he just stayed home from school that day and pretended to be sick? It wasn't all that hard to look and act sick if he really tried.

All this thinking was hard work. It was time to take a break from the homework and the heavy thinking, so Dan headed to the kitchen for some pop and chips. Maybe a little junk food would help him decide what to do about Mrs. Henderson.

If you were Dan, and you had to choose, what would *you* do? Why?

More to think about:

Do you think Mrs. Henderson is just a mean person?

Why do you think Dan wants to give Mrs. Henderson a card?

How do you think Mrs. Henderson will feel if no one in the class gives her anything on Valentine's Day?

Why should Dan care how Mrs. Henderson feels?

Do you think Dan should go along with his class or do what he believes is right?

Double the Money

Tara wiped her forehead with the end of her shirt and sat back on her heels. The garden looked great, if she did say so herself. This was the second summer she had helped Mrs. Miller with her garden and she was beginning to feel like a "pro."

At the start, Tara didn't know a weed from a flower or an annual from a perennial. Now Mrs. Miller let her take care of the garden all by herself. It was a good feeling to know that Mrs. Miller trusted her to do a good job.

While she hung her garden tools on the hooks in Mrs. Miller's garage, Tara thought about the ten-speed bike she was going to buy with the money she earned. She had been saving for almost a year to buy a bike. Her older brother Mickey already had a great bike.

The police department was having their annual auction in two weeks, and she planned to have all the money she needed by then.

Tara was still thinking about her bike when she collected her money for the work she had done. Mrs. Miller apologized for having to pay Tara in one-dollar bills, but that was all she had left after her shopping trip.

Tara thanked Mrs. Miller and stuffed the bills into her shirt pocket. As soon as she got home, she unfolded the bills so she could add them to the rest of her savings. That's when she discovered that Mrs. Miller had given her eight one-dollar bills and a ten-dollar bill instead of nine ones.

Tara was so excited. She really lucked out. Double the money for one job! It meant she could use that ten toward her bike, and she was sure Mrs. Miller would never even miss it.

But then Tara started thinking about how Mrs. Miller trusted her with the garden work. Did she want to take a chance on losing that trust for ten dollars? How much was trust worth?

But a bike was a bike. She had never wanted anything as much as she wanted that ten-speed. There were only two more weeks before the auction. She really needed that extra money.

Tara knew what her brother Mickey would do. He would return the ten immediately. He wouldn't even think about keeping it. He would just bike right back to Mrs. Miller's and return the money.

But he already had a bike. Tara was the one who really needed that money, and she just knew that she would appreciate the money a lot more than Mrs. Miller. Mrs. Miller would probably just use it to buy more groceries.

If Tara did return the money, maybe she could ask Mrs. Miller if she could earn back the ten by doing some extra jobs. But what if Mrs. Miller didn't have any extra jobs? Then Tara would lose the money, and Mrs.

Miller would receive a ten-dollar bill she didn't even know she had. It just didn't seem fair.

Tara thought about her best friend, Lindsey. She was sure that Lindsey would tell her to "go for it." Lindsey would tell her that it would be crazy for her not to keep the money.

Tara knew exactly what her parents would say. They would tell her to do what she knew was right. But weren't there ever special exceptions? Like when you really wanted something the way she wanted that bike? All her friends had ten-speeds. Her brother had a ten-speed. Probably everyone in the world had a ten-speed. Except her. Tara had never wanted anything the way she wanted that bike, but she also knew that she hadn't really earned the extra money.

If you were Tara, and you had to choose, what would *you* do? Why?

More to think about:

Why does Mrs. Miller trust Tara?

Why would Tara's brother return the money without a second thought?

Why do you think Tara's friend Lindsey would keep the money?

Should it count for anything that Tara really wants the bike and has been saving a very long time to get it?

Everybody's Doing It

"I can get you a copy of next week's final math exam for just five bucks." That was Kyle's message when he cornered Todd in the gym after basketball practice.

Todd had told Kyle he wasn't interested, but that was yesterday. Since then several of the other guys on the team had let him know what they thought. Some said, "Lighten up and join the real world." Others urged him not to be a loser. Some of the guys were even making chicken sounds when they passed him in the hall.

Todd knew what his teammates were doing was wrong, but he sure didn't want to end up losing his friends over this. If he didn't join them, he could end up with no friends at all.

Todd figured that there must be some kids who hadn't bought the exam; but if Kyle was right, Todd was the only guy in the whole fifth grade who was holding out.

Todd had to admit that math was his hardest subject and he could use all the help he could get. Besides, what was so wrong with buying a copy of the exam as long as everyone else already had one anyway? He could pretend it was a math review sheet and still study all the other stuff he would have studied if he didn't have a copy of the exam. That way, he could get a better grade on the final exam and he wouldn't risk losing any of his friends.

But what if everyone did so well on the exam that their math teacher, Mr. Carlson, got wise? What if Mr. Carlson found out that they had all cheated? Then what?

Todd shuddered. Mr. Carlson would tell Mr. Hanson, the principal. Then Mr. Hanson would want to see all the parents, and that would be just the beginning.

Todd opened his locker door and stared at his math book. What did he really want to do?

Did he really want to cheat? No.

Did he want to get a good score on his math final? Yes.

Did he want to lose all his friends by not going along with what they were doing? No.

Did he want to do something he might regret later? No.

So where did that leave him? He didn't want to cheat, but he wanted to get a good grade on his math exam.

Todd could still get some extra help from Mr. Carlson or one of the math tutors. He could always turn the TV off earlier at night and spend more time on his math. That wasn't the easy way, but it was one of his choices.

What about Kyle and the other guys who were going to cheat? If he didn't buy the exam, they were probably going to give him a rough time or else avoid him like the plague. Maybe both. They might give him a rough time and then avoid him for the rest of the school year.

It also meant they would all do better on the math exam than he would. Probably a lot better. How would he feel then—sorry that he hadn't cheated, too?

No matter what he did, he might have a lot to lose. He wasn't sure what he should do.

If you were Todd, and you had to choose, what would *you* do? Why?

More to think about:

Is Todd correct in thinking that most of the kids in his class are going to cheat?

How would you say Todd and his classmates view cheating?

Why do you think Kyle is giving Todd such a hard time?

Is Todd wrong if he chooses not to go along with his friends? Would your answer be the same if he's the *only* kid in the fifth grade who decides not to buy the exam? Why?

If Todd goes along with everyone else and buys a copy of the exam, does that make his decision right?

Is Todd all out of options?

Finders Keepers?

Tony and his friend Leon chained their bikes to the metal posts of the bicycle rack and zipped up their matching sweatshirts.

Saturday morning at the neighborhood park was the best part of the whole week. The swings were still empty, they had the jungle gym to themselves, and there were only a couple runners on the jogging trail.

They were just warming up on the jogging path when a jogger in a bright blue warmup suit passed them. As he jogged by with his earphones clamped to his head, he waved to the boys.

Tony and Leon watched as the jogger rounded the curve ahead. That's when they saw something fall out of the pocket of his warmup suit, so they sprinted over to investigate.

There, big as life, was a twenty-dollar bill. Tony started to call out to the jogger, but Leon jabbed him hard in the ribs and told him to think again. Leon picked up the money and grinned at Tony. "This is our lucky day, and you were about to blow it. With this little piece of paper here we can have a blast at the video arcade. Let's grab our bikes and head on over there, so we're there when they open."

Tony's first thought was to catch up with the jogger and return the money, but by now the man was completely out of sight. They would have to hurry if they were going to find him before he left the park.

Leon told Tony to forget about the jogger. "That guy probably won't even miss the money. He'd probably spend it on a pizza or something and not even think anything about it. We'll get a lot more fun out of it than he ever would."

Leon wadded up the bill and stuffed it into the back pocket of his jeans. As he headed back toward the bicycle rack, he yelled for Tony to hurry up. He wasn't going to wait all day.

It seemed that things were pretty much out of Tony's hands. Leon had the money and the jogger was nowhere to be seen. Leon had his mind set on spending the money, with or without Tony.

Tony could still try to find the jogger and tell him about the lost money. But if Leon took off with the money, then Tony wouldn't have any money to give back to the jogger and, by the time he found the man, Leon would already be living it up at the video arcade.

Tony kicked an empty pop can off the jogging path and headed back to the bicycle rack to find Leon. What if he insisted that the two of them track down the jogger and return the money? That was what he really wanted to do, but Tony knew that Leon already had his mind made up. He was going to spend the money.

Leon had the money stuffed safely away in his pocket and he wasn't about to give it up, not without a fight anyway. Tony wasn't about to get into a fight with his best friend over someone else's twenty bucks.

So what if Tony just refused to go with Leon to spend the money? Then Leon would have a good time and Tony would be stuck with nothing to do for the rest of the day.

Tony wanted to do the right thing, but if he couldn't convince Leon to give back the money, he didn't know what he would do. Leon could be pretty stubborn when he really wanted something.

If you were Tony, and you had to choose, what would *you* do? Why?

More to think about:

If you were the jogger, what would you want Tony and Leon to do?

What do you think of Leon's reason for keeping the money?

Do you think Tony is going to be able to convince Leon to return the money?

Why doesn't Tony want to keep the money?

Would it change anything if Tony and Leon had found the money just lying on the side of the path without knowing where it came from? Why?

47

Good News, Bad News

Leslie counted the money again. Counting both the checks and the cash, the pledges came to over eighty dollars for the walk for World Hunger sponsored by her church. That was the good news.

The bad news was that she had collected all her pledges *before* the walk. When Leslie had asked people for pledges, she had told everyone that five miles was nothing. That she could walk twice that without even working up a sweat.

Everyone believed her and paid their pledges before the walk instead of waiting until after she finished. She had received pledge money from Ms. Emerson, her fourth-grade teacher; from Ms. Franklin, the school counselor; and even from Mr. Hanson, the school principal. Then there were her mom and dad, her uncle, and her grandparents. Even Mr. Baker from next door and Mrs. Jackson from down the street had given her money.

How was Leslie to know that her sister Niki was going to twist her ankle before they had even walked two miles?

Leslie didn't want to leave her little sister sitting at a rest stop by herself until Dad picked her up, so Leslie waited with Niki while a paramedic checked the ankle and they called their home.

After Dad arrived to pick up Niki, there was still time for Leslie to finish the walk. But Niki wanted Leslie to go to the doctor with her, so Leslie stayed with her sister.

By the time the doctor had taped the ankle and Niki was back home resting on the couch, it was too late for Leslie to finish the walk.

Now Leslie had a big problem. She had already collected her pledge money, but she had not finished the walk. What should she do? Should she return all or part of the money? Or should she keep the money and give it to the World Hunger Drive as planned?

After all, the money was for people who really needed the food. It wasn't like she would be keeping the money to spend on herself or anything.

But her pledge was her promise to do something. And she had not done what she promised to do.

Talking to her uncle and her grandparents would be easy. She knew that they would agree with her parents: she should keep the money and give it to the hunger drive.

But what about everyone else? It would be easy to pretend that she had finished the walk. She could just give the money to her church and save everyone a lot of hassle. That way Leslie wouldn't have to do a lot of explaining about her sister's ankle, and she wouldn't end up looking foolish.

But what if Leslie didn't tell everyone about not finishing the walk and they found out later? Would they ever trust her again? That was something to think about.

Ms. Emerson was her favorite teacher and Mr. Baker was always helping her get her cat Amber down out of his big tree. And Mrs. Jackson was always dropping by with freshly baked chocolate chip cookies.

Leslie wanted to do the right thing, but she didn't want to have to do a lot of explaining either.

If you were Leslie, and you had to choose, what would *you* do? Why?

More to think about:

Do you think Leslie did the right thing by going with her sister to the doctor, or do you think she should have finished the walk?

Would Leslie's sponsors want to know that she didn't finish the walk?

Do you think any of Leslie's sponsors will ask her to return their money if she tells them why she didn't finish her walk? How do you think they will feel about the promise she made?

Is it ever right to break a promise?

Green, Green Everywhere

Kathleen Kelly loved St. Patrick's Day. It was one of her favorite holidays. Her mom was Irish. Her dad was Irish. And her grandparents were Irish. Just about everyone in her family was Irish. Even her dog was an Irish setter.

Kathleen was proud of being Irish, and she loved to wear green on St. Patrick's Day to show everyone how proud she was.

But last year, in third grade, she had worn green on St. Patrick's Day, and it had not been a good day. In fact, it had been a very bad day, one of the worst days of her life.

She had worn a green skirt and green sweater, green socks, and she had even brought green sugar cookies for her class.

Everyone else in her class had worn green, too, but not as much green as Kathleen. Billy told her she looked dumb in all that green. Kurt told her that all that green made him want to throw up. And Pam told her that her green sugar cookies were stupid. Some of the kids even teased her about her Irish name.

Kathleen never wanted to go through another day like that again. Ever.

She teased her friend Charlie once about his big ears, but that was different. He knew that she still liked him even if he did have big ears.

But tomorrow was another St. Patrick's Day. And she had to decide what to wear. She pulled out every drawer in her dresser looking for something to wear that wouldn't look dumb or stupid.

She finally decided on jeans, a blue sweater, and white socks. And no way was she going to take any cookies this year. Kathleen wasn't even going to wear her grandmother's shamrock pin. This year no one was going to tease her about being Irish.

Kathleen looked at the shamrock pin lying there in her jewelry box. Grandma Charlotte had given it to her on her birthday two years ago and it had always been one of Kathleen's special treasures. The pin reminded her of all the wonderful stories Grandma Charlotte used to tell about growing up in Ireland. But it also reminded her of one of the worst days of her entire life.

Kathleen wondered what Grandma Charlotte would do if she were in her place. Kathleen knew what she would do. Grandma would wear green because she was proud of her Irish heritage and she would want the whole world to know.

Kathleen wanted to show everyone that she was proud of being Irish, too, but she sure didn't want to end up feeling dumb again. And she sure didn't want everyone making jokes about her all day long.

What could she do? She could always stay home from school and pretend she was sick. That would be the safe thing to do, and the easiest thing to do. That way she could wear whatever she wanted to wear and no one would even know.

But Kathleen knew that wasn't what her Grandma Charlotte would do. Grandma would march to school proudly wearing the green—probably a lot of green.

What if Kathleen did go to school but wore just a little green? She could wear a green sweater with her jeans and white socks. And maybe her shamrock pin, too. That way she'd look pretty much like all the other kids and no one would make fun of her.

Or she could wear no green at all. She could just pretend it was no special day and wear her jeans and blue sweater. That way she would not get teased again.

If you were Kathleen, and you had to choose, what would *you* do? Why?

More to think about:

Why did the other kids tease Kathleen about wearing so much green?

Kathleen still remembers the teasing a year later. Why do you think it's still on her mind?

Why would Grandma Charlotte take the chance of being teased just to wear the green?

Have you ever teased someone about something they wore or the way they looked?

How do you feel when someone makes fun of you?

His Brother's Keeper?

Rob stared at the sign on his brother Gordon's bedroom door. "KEEP OUT! THIS MEANS YOU!" He should have paid more attention to that sign two days ago.

Rob just wanted to borrow one of Gordon's giant erasers for his math homework. He knew Gordon kept his sketching pencils and erasers safely tucked away in an old leather case in the bottom of his shirt drawer along with the rest of his sketching materials.

Rob found the case, but there were no erasers in it. Instead, there were little plastic bags of what looked like tobacco or old tea leaves. It didn't take a rocket scientist to figure out that the little bags were filled with marijuana.

Rob stuck the case back in the drawer and didn't say anything to anyone about what he had found.

What do you say to an older brother in junior high? "Gee, Gordon, is that really marijuana you've got stashed in that old leather case?" Or maybe, "Hey, man, what's up? Smoked any good pot lately?"

Yeah, right. There was no way Rob was going to come right out and tell his brother what he knew. You just don't tell big brothers what to do. Gordon had heard all the same lectures Rob had about the dangers of smoking marijuana. Rob even had the printed handouts the police had given Ms. Terry's fourth-grade health class sitting there big as life on the hall table where he had left them.

Rob wanted to do something to help Gordon, but what could he do? Maybe he could write an anonymous note to Mom? "Dear Mrs. Danton: Did you know your oldest son is using pot?" Yeah, right. Like she wouldn't recognize his handwriting or anything.

Rob considered talking to Dad when he saw him on the weekend. "Say, Dad, I think there's something you should know about Gordon. I think he's smoking pot and I don't know what else."

And what would Dad do? First, he would yell at Rob since Rob was there and Gordon wasn't. Then Dad would have it out with Gordon. There would be a lot of yelling and shouting, and Gordon would be grounded for the rest of his life! But that wouldn't be the end of it. Gordon would come after Rob. If he was lucky, Gordon would just tell him to mind his own business. No way was Rob getting off that easy: Gordon would punch him out and probably never speak to him again. You just don't squeal on your older brother.

Rob could talk to Mom, but he would have the same problem if he talked to her. She would probably cry a lot first before she got mad. You just don't rat on your own brother. You don't talk to the counselor at school either. You just keep your mouth shut if you know what's good for you.

Wasn't that what Gordon always told him? "Keep your mouth shut and your hands in your pockets and you'll stay out of trouble." Rob wasn't sure exactly what that meant, but he figured it meant he should mind his own business.

Besides, maybe smoking a little marijuana now and then wasn't any big deal anyway. It wasn't like Gordon was into cocaine or heroin or anything really bad.

What had that police officer said in Ms. Terry's health class? Marijuana often leads to using the hard drugs and that the hard drugs often lead to a life of crime and violence, sometimes even death.

Rob sure didn't want his brother to end up in serious trouble, but what could Rob do to help Gordon without ending up in trouble himself?

It was really Gordon's problem, not his. After all, it wasn't Rob's responsibility to keep his brother out of trouble, or was it?

If you were Rob, and you had to choose, what would *you* do? Why?

More to think about:

Why do you suppose Gordon is smoking marijuana?

Why is Rob so worried about his brother?

Why would Mom and Dad be so upset if Rob tells them what he found?

Does Gordon have any reason to be upset with Rob?

If Only . . .

Brian watched his sister, Margaret, twirl around the living room in her pink toe slippers. She was twelve and she spent most of her life prancing around on her toes telling everyone she was going to be a famous ballerina someday.

He was going to tell her about the accident, but then at the last minute he chickened out. Maybe he'd tell her tomorrow. Older sisters could be a real pain sometimes. They always thought they knew everything.

Brian hadn't meant to ruin her book. It had just happened. He took the book out of his shirt drawer and looked at it again. It was called *Ballet Made Easy*, only now the ballerina on the cover had a streak of mustard running through her hair and all the way down her leg.

It wasn't like he meant to drop his hot dog on the book or anything. His sister shouldn't have left it sitting on the kitchen counter in the first place.

He tried wiping the mustard off the book with a kitchen sponge, but that just spread the mustard around even more. And now the ballerina looked pretty silly with yellow mustard streaks.

Brian was going to tell Margaret about the book right away, but he knew she would yell and scream the way she always did whenever anything went wrong.

Then it occurred to him that he could hide the book and she might not miss it for weeks. Maybe months. And by the time she found the book, he could just pretend not to know anything about it. There was a lot to be said for taking the easy way out where Margaret the grouch was concerned.

He remembered last summer when he accidentally broke a string on her tennis racket. He didn't mean to break the string. How was he to know her tennis racket was in such bad shape? The way she carried on, you would have thought she had lost her best friend. Good grief, all she had to do was get the racket restrung. It wasn't like he had wrecked the racket forever or anything.

Brian sure didn't want to go through anything like that ever again. There had to be some way out of this mess.

Maybe he could save his allowance and buy her a new book before she ever missed the old book. But a book that big probably cost a lot, and it could take him a lifetime to save up that much money.

Maybe he could do some extra jobs around the house or help Dad in the yard to earn the money for the book. He might even help Mom in the garden or help Dad paint the front porch. He didn't really want to take on any extra work, but doing a few jobs was a lot easier than having to deal with Margaret's bad moods.

Really the whole mess was Margaret's fault. If only she hadn't left the book sitting on the kitchen counter, he never would have spilled mustard on it. And if she had put the book back in her room where it belonged, neither of them would have a problem now. The kitchen was a place for food, not books. She should be lucky he wasn't eating spaghetti when it happened.

Brian wanted to do the right thing, but he didn't want to listen to Margaret's moaning and groaning if he didn't have to. There just had to be some way of avoiding a big scene with her.

If you were Brian, and you had to choose, what would *you* do? Why?

More to think about:

Why do you think Margaret got so upset when Brian broke a string on her tennis racket?

What do you think of Brian's ideas for replacing the book so he doesn't have to tell his sister about the accident?

Why do you think Brian would rather try to replace the book than admit the accident to his sister?

Is Brian right to think that Margaret is at least partly to blame for the accident?

Korean Eyes

Kim is new to Nathan's second-grade class this year. In fact, she is new to America. She arrived last summer from a placed called Korea and is just learning English.

Kim lives just down the street from Nathan and takes the same school bus he does. He doesn't sit next to her on the bus, because she's a *girl*—and he never sits next to any *girls*. No one sits next to Kim. She always sits alone.

During recess Kim plays by herself in the playground sandbox. When she tried to use the swings, an older kid from the fifth grade told her she couldn't use them because she was a "Chink," whatever that means.

Then there was a kid in Nathan's class named Joey who made fun of Kim's eyes. He told her to open her eyes and maybe she could see something. Everyone in the class laughed when he said that. But then Ms. Jackson came in and the whole class stopped laughing and the room got very quiet.

At lunchtime on Wednesday, Ms. Jackson asked if someone would take Kim to the lunchroom, so she wouldn't have to eat by herself. No one volunteered, so Ms. Jackson took Kim herself.

By the end of the first week of school, most of the second-graders had made friends—but not Kim. She still rode the bus alone, played by herself in the sandbox at recess, and ate lunch by herself.

Friday afternoon Ms. Jackson had a surprise for her class. She introduced a young woman named Kathryn who was on the U.S. Olympic ice skating team. Kathryn told the class how she and her family had come to the United States from Japan when she was five years old. She also talked about how hard it was for her to make friends because she couldn't speak much English, and how the other kids did not want to play with her.

Kathryn told Nathan's class about a girl named Nancy who lived in her neighborhood. Nancy invited Kathryn to her house to play and they soon became special friends. She told them how important it is for everyone to have a friend and how she hoped that everyone in Ms. Jackson's class had a friend.

Then Kathryn told them stories about how hard she trained for the Olympics and how proud she was to be part of the U.S. team even though she had been born in another country. She said that Americans were very special because they accept people for who they are and not because of the way they look or talk.

When Kathryn was finished speaking to the class, everyone clapped for a long time and asked for her autograph. After she left, Ms. Jackson asked the class if they had learned anything from Kathryn that they might use in their class.

Jimmy raised his hand and said that he had learned how important it is to work hard for what you want.

Ms. Jackson agreed that that was important, but had they learned anything else?

Marcus raised his hand and said that he had learned how important it is to be a friend. Especially to someone who doesn't have a friend.

The class was still talking about Kathryn when school ended for the day. Everyone rushed to their coat hooks to grab their jackets.

Ms. Jackson helped Kim on with her jacket and then asked the class if anyone would like to help Kim find her school bus.

If you were Nathan, and you had to choose, what would *you* do? Why?

More to think about:

Why do you think Ms. Jackson wants members of Nathan's class to eat lunch with Kim and help her in other ways?

Why do you think Ms. Jackson invited Kathryn to speak to her class?

How do you think Kim is feeling about her new school and her new country?

Why do you think some of the other kids were teasing Kim?

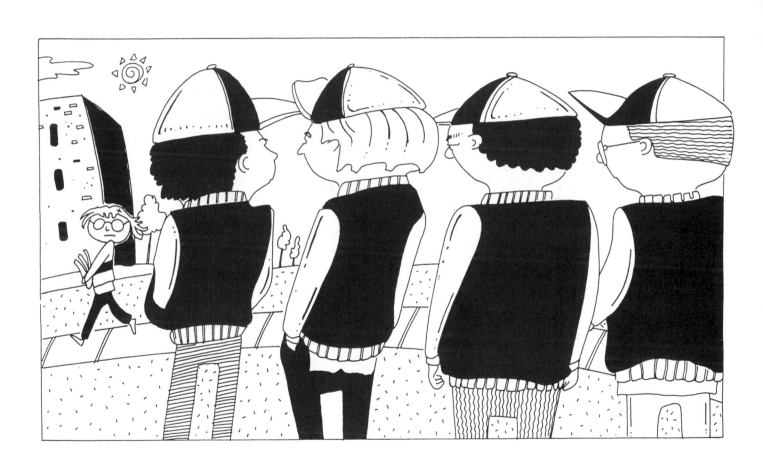

New Guys Around

Tanya was playing tag with her friends on the school playground when she saw the guys in the blue jackets again. This was the third day she had seen them.

There were four of them and they all wore blue athletic jackets and matching baseball caps. She knew they didn't go to her school, but they could be from the high school down the street.

Tanya had not paid much attention to the boys when she saw them on Monday. But when she saw them again on Tuesday, she began to watch them more carefully. Now they were back on Wednesday. That was three days in a row.

It looked like they were selling or trading something to some of the sixth-graders. Tanya was looking forward to being a sixth-grader herself next year. The sixth-graders got to go on more field trips than the fifth-graders and the sixth-graders got to have their own class song.

Tanya ran behind a huge oak tree while Cassie tried to tag Marsha.

Then Cassie turned suddenly and started after Tanya. Tanya took off toward the basketball hoops where the boys in the blue jackets were, but they moved off toward the soccer field.

Tanya stopped running and Cassie tagged her. Then both girls fell down where they were, gasping for breath and laughing so hard that tears ran down their cheeks. Cassie was up on her feet and running again before Tanya could tag her.

Tanya chased after Cassie, but before she could tag anyone else, the school bell rang. Back in class, she watched Mr. Fisher pull down the map of the United States and point to the state capitals with his plastic ruler.

While the rest of the class called out the names of the state capitals, Tanya was still thinking about the boys in the blue jackets.

What if they were selling drugs to the sixth-graders? If they were really selling drugs, then she knew she should tell someone.

But that could get her into a lot of trouble with the sixth-graders— at least some of them. They would probably find a way to get even with her. She didn't even want to think about it.

It was better to keep her nose out of their business and just let them do their own thing. But what if the guys in the blue jackets started trying to sell to the younger kids? Like her brother, Billy, in the third grade. How would she feel then if she didn't do something to stop them?

But what if she was getting all steamed up over nothing? Maybe those guys were just trading football cards or baseball cards. Boy, would she be embarrassed if she made a big deal out of nothing.

Somehow she knew that the guys in the blue jackets were not just trading cards. The way they kept to themselves and moved away when Tanya and her friends approached, she was pretty sure that they were doing something they weren't supposed to be doing.

Mr. Fisher was asking what the capital of Michigan was. Tanya knew the answer, but she was still trying to figure out the answer to her own problem.

Should she risk looking like a jerk and tell someone about her suspicions? Or should she just forget about the whole thing and mind her own business?

If you were Tanya, and you had to choose, what would *you* do? Why?

More to think about:

What do you think the boys in the blue jackets are doing?

What do you think Tanya's friends Marsha and Cassie would tell her to do?

Tanya seems very concerned about what the sixth-graders would think if she reports what she saw. Should she be?

Why should being embarrassed or looking silly matter to Tanya if she really believes something wrong is going on?

If the guys in the blue jackets knew what Tanya is thinking about them, what do you suppose they would say to her?

No Easy Answers

Lynn had worked hard on her math homework all Saturday afternoon and had finally finished it. Math was her hardest subject and she had spent a lot of time and effort trying to get all her percentages to come out right. She was just putting her assignment into her math folder for Monday when the telephone rang. It was her friend Beth.

Beth told Lynn that she needed the answers to the math problems because she wouldn't have time to do them herself. She had a dance recital that night and she still had to finish studying for the spelling test. Then Sunday she was spending the day with her dad and they would probably be going to the zoo, so she wouldn't be home till late. Too late to do any math.

Lynn didn't want to give Beth the answers to the problems she had worked so hard on all afternoon. She had not gone roller skating with her sister just so she could finish them.

Lynn felt like telling her friend to take her math homework to her dad's on Sunday and get him to help her. She could go to the zoo some other time. Or she could come home early on Sunday and work on her math then.

Beth was still talking about her busy schedule. "I just won't have time to do those problems and you know how hard math is for me. It would take me forever to figure out all those answers. I really need your help."

Lynn was still trying to think of a way to tell Beth she didn't want to give her the answers, but Beth was busy trying to convince Lynn that she had to do it.

"I would give *you* the answers if you asked me. You know I would. That's what friends are for. So you've just got to give me the answers. I'll even treat you to a sausage pizza next Saturday if you help me out. Please, just this once?"

Lynn knew it would be easy enough just to give Beth the answers. After all, she was one of Lynn's best friends and friends were supposed to help each other. Lynn knew she would never hear the end of it if she didn't help her friend out. And Beth would probably tell everyone in their class how Lynn had refused to help her.

But Lynn had figured out the answers to those problems all by herself and no one had helped *her*. It just wasn't fair that Beth was asking her to do something she didn't want to do.

What if she didn't help Beth? She might just lose a friend; she had to admit that Beth had always been there for her when she had needed her.

Beth had dropped her homework off every day for a whole week when Lynn had the flu last month. Beth always saved her a seat on the school bus every morning. And Beth had even loaned her lunch money last Friday when Lynn had forgotten her lunch bag.

Lynn knew what she wanted to do. She wanted to tell Beth that she couldn't give her the answers because it just wasn't the right thing to do.

But she couldn't seem to get the words out. Her mouth felt dry and she just stared at the phone.

Beth stopped snapping her bubble gum and asked again. "So can you give me the answers to those math problems before I have to go get ready for my recital? I really need them."

If you were Lynn, and you had to choose, what would *you* do? Why?

More to think about:

Why do you think Lynn really does not want to give Beth the answers?

What are Beth's reasons for wanting the homework answers? Do you think they are good reasons?

How much should it matter to Lynn that Beth might tell their friends that Lynn wouldn't give her the answers?

What would their math teacher say if she heard their conversation?

Out in Left Field

Heather slammed the front door behind her and headed for the kitchen. She knew what she was going to do. She was going to drop out of that stupid gym class tomorrow as soon as she got to school.

She grabbed the milk carton from the refrigerator and the peanut butter jar from the cupboard. Then she smeared the peanut butter on her bread while she thought again about her gym class.

There she was stuck in left field. Again. Out in left field, the only thing she ever saw were a lot of dandelions. And sometimes a butterfly if she was lucky.

Heather loved softball. Last year, in the third grade, Ms. Wilson had let her play first base. During almost every gym class she got to play first base. But that was *last* year.

This year there was a new gym teacher—Ms. Carter. And this year Heather got stuck in left field almost every day. No one ever hit a ball past second base, so she was out there all by herself just watching the grass grow.

Heather was sure Ms. Carter didn't like her. If she liked her, she'd let her play first base.

Heather knew what her dad would say. He would tell her how important it was to be a "team player." Well, how could she be a team player if she never saw any action?

Heather was sure her mom would tell her the same thing. She'd tell her that every position on the team was important, and that you work your way up to a better position by doing a good job where you are.

Well, Heather had news for her mom: if you never got to get your hands on the ball, then how can you ever show anyone what you can really do?

It was just like last year when Heather wanted to be in the class play. Instead, she got stuck painting giant trees and flowers. She spent hours painting trees and flowers. She knew someone had to do it, but why her?

And how about in second grade, when she wanted to be an angel in the Christmas play at church. And she was stuck being a shepherd. She even had to carry a toy lamb in her arms. Boy, did she feel dumb.

Heather poured herself some more milk and then headed up to her sister's room. Cindy was in the sixth grade and sometimes it was easier for Heather to talk to Cindy than to their mom or dad. Cindy still knew what it was like to be a kid.

Heather explained her problem while Cindy worked on her science project for the science fair. Cindy just listened until Heather was done. Then she smiled.

"That sounds like last year when I wanted to be on the track team and Jennifer got the spot I wanted."

"So what did you do? Did you stop talking to Jennifer?"

Cindy shook her head. "Nope, it wasn't Jennifer's fault that she was better at the Four-Forty than I was. I just kept practicing with the track team every day and I kept improving my time. That's probably why this year I made the team. If it's something you really want to do, then don't give up. Just keep doing it until you're doing it as well as you possibly can."

Heather shook her head. That wasn't really what she wanted Cindy to say. She was sure Cindy was going to tell her to drop off the team or ask to change to a different gym class or complain to Ms. Carter. Now Heather wasn't sure what she should do.

If you were Heather, and you had to choose, what would *you* do? Why?

More to think about:

Do you think Ms. Carter doesn't like Heather?

What does it mean to be a "team player"?

What do you think about Cindy's advice?

What might happen if Heather leaves the softball team? What might happen if she changes teams?

Ready, Aim, Fire!

Carol wasn't in school today, so Jamie joined Rita and some of her friends for lunch in the school cafeteria. They were halfway through their lunch when some boys at another table began throwing food at them.

Then some of Rita's friends began throwing food back at the boys. French fries, pickles, and carrot sticks were flying through the air and soon there was a real mess on the tables, on the walls, and on the floor.

The cafeteria supervisor, Ms. Marsh, called in Mr. Hanson, the school principal. When Mr. Hanson saw the mess, he was furious.

Mr. Hanson ordered all the kids at both tables to clean up the mess. Then he told them that they would not be allowed to return to school the next day unless they brought their parents to school to meet with him.

Mr. Hanson signed a pink slip for each of the kids to give to their parents. Jamie stared at her pink slip. It just wasn't fair. She had not actually thrown any food. And she did not want to have to bring either of her parents to school to talk to Mr. Hanson. She did not even want to tell her parents about the food fight.

The rest of the day seemed to drag on forever. When Jamie finally got home, she gave her dog, Scamper, a big hug and then went right up to her room to think about what happened.

She didn't do anything wrong, but she also didn't try to stop anyone from throwing the food. Did that make her as guilty as the rest of them?

Jamie's mom was a single parent now that her dad was living by himself in his own apartment. Jamie saw him on weekends, but her mother was the one who would have to talk to Mr. Hanson.

Her mom had her hands full just working and taking care of the house and the kids. Her mom didn't need any more problems. But Jamie couldn't go back to school unless her mother saw Mr. Hanson, so it looked like she didn't have much choice. She had to tell her mother.

Jamie took Mr. Hanson's pink note out of her book bag and looked at it again. The note wasn't going to disappear and neither was the problem. Jamie had to decide what to do and she had to decide fast. It was almost time for dinner and her mother would want to know all about her day.

Jamie thought about calling her friend Carol and asking her what to do. But Carol hadn't even been there, so she probably wouldn't be much help. In a way, it was all Carol's fault. If Carol had been at school, then Jamie would have been sitting with her as usual and not with Rita and her friends. Then there wouldn't even be a problem.

What if she just told Mr. Hanson how she really felt. She hadn't done anything wrong and she didn't think she should be punished for something she didn't do.

But she had to admit that she didn't get up and leave the table when the food fight began. And she didn't really tell them to stop. In fact, it had been kind of exciting for a few minutes until she saw how angry Mr. Hanson was.

And what if she didn't receive the same punishment as Rita and her friends? Would the other kids be mad at her?

This looked like one of those "Lose-Lose" situations. No matter what she did, someone was going to end up very unhappy.

Jamie had no idea what she was going to do. She heard her mother calling her for dinner, so it looked like she had just run out of time.

If you were Jamie, and you had to choose, what would *you* do? Why?

More to think about:

Do you think Jamie's problem is really Carol's fault?

Do you think Mr. Hanson is being fair when he asks *all* the kids at both tables to bring their parents to school?

Do you think Jamie should be treated the same as the other kids who actually threw the food?

How do you think Jamie's mother is going to react if Jamie tells her about the problem?

How would things have been different if Jamie tried to stop the food fight?

Robot-Girl

Stephanie was in Kristi's class in school, but she didn't belong to Kristi's special group of friends, so Kristi hardly ever talked to her. In fact, no one talked much to Stephanie unless there was no one else to talk to. Just about all the kids in the third grade thought she looked "weird."

Stephanie wore very thick glasses, a hearing aid, and she even had a thick metal brace on one leg.

Some of the kids made fun of her and told jokes about her behind her back. They said she looked like a robot. Some kids even called her "Robot-Girl" right to her face.

The last day before Christmas vacation, Stephanie was absent from school and Ms. Thomas explained that she was home sick with the flu. Then Ms. Thomas asked if someone in class would volunteer to take Stephanie's homework to her, so she wouldn't get too far behind the rest of the class.

No one volunteered. Instead, everyone just snickered and looked the other way. Kristi began to feel very uncomfortable because Ms. Thomas was waiting for someone to volunteer, and Kristi knew that no one would.

Kristi wanted to volunteer, but she could just see all the other kids staring at her if she did. She was sure they would make jokes about her later, behind her back. She wanted to help Stephanie but not if it meant being teased by the other kids. Kristi wanted to raise her hand, but her arm seemed like it was glued to her desk.

She knew where Stephanie lived, and Kristi was sure her mom wouldn't mind stopping by Stephanie's to drop off the homework. Maybe she could talk to Ms. Thomas after class and offer to take Stephanie's homework to her. No one in the class would know, and there would be no jokes about her being a friend of "Robot-Girl."

It wasn't that Kristi didn't want to be Stephanie's friend. She just didn't want to end up losing her own friends by doing a favor for someone she hardly knew.

If no one volunteered, Ms. Thomas would probably just drop off the homework herself. Stephanie wasn't going to suffer or anything. Besides, Ms. Thomas was the teacher. Wasn't it her job anyway to drop off the homework?

Why should Kristi worry about Stephanie? She didn't even know her. All Kristi knew was that Stephanie had something wrong with her muscles. Kristi had never asked her about her problem. She had just stayed away, like all the other kids in class.

Maybe Stephanie's mother could pick up the homework. All Ms. Thomas had to do was call Stephanie's house and that would take care of everything.

Kristi looked around the classroom at the other kids. The room was so quiet that she could hear Byron's heavy breathing behind her. He had asthma and she could always tell when he was having a problem. His breathing got louder and rougher. Sometimes he even wheezed when he tried to talk. But at least he didn't look weird or anything.

The final bell was about to ring and Kristi still didn't know what she was going to do. She wanted to help, but she didn't want to raise her hand in front of everyone.

Ms. Thomas stood waiting by her desk with Stephanie's homework papers in her hand.

If you were Kristi, and you had to choose, what would *you* do? Why?

More to think about:

Why do you think the kids ignore Stephanie?

Why don't the kids ignore Byron?

How do you think Stephanie feels about the way the other kids treat her?

What do you think will happen to Stephanie if the kids keep ignoring her?

What makes Kristi feel that she should volunteer?

What seems to be stopping Kristi from raising her hand to take Stephanie her homework?

Sticks and Stones

"Hey, Fatso, don't sit on that bench. You might squash it. If my dog was that fat, I'd trade him in for a cow."

Then another kid joined in. "Hey, I hear there's still time to enter the pig competition at the state fair. Do you want me to sign you up?"

Everyone on the playground was laughing. Everyone except Ryan. He picked up his cap and walked slowly back to the school building, mumbling, "Sticks and stones can break my bones, but names can never hurt me."

But Andy knew different. Names do hurt. He laughed with the other kids because he didn't know what else to do, but he really didn't feel like laughing.

He was remembering when giant red bumps broke out all over his body. The doctor called them hives and told him they were an allergic reaction to some medicine he was taking. Andy just called them a DISASTER.

The other kids called him "Bumps" and no one wanted to play with him, because they didn't want to get what he had. That whole week he had to play by himself on the playground. He ate his lunch alone in the cloak-room with all the boots and jackets just so the kids in the cafeteria wouldn't give him a hard time.

By the end of the week the bumps had gone and his friends were starting to play with him again. It had been like a bad dream. A very bad dream. He still remembered how it felt to be laughed at and avoided by the other kids.

Andy thought about Ryan heading back to the classroom by himself, or more likely to the candy machine in the cafeteria.

Andy's mom was always on some kind of diet. She claimed the more worried or upset she was, the more she ate. Boy, if that was really true, then Andy figured Ryan could end up bigger than a blimp before he was even out of fourth grade the way the kids teased him all the time.

Andy was sure glad it was Ryan's problem. Andy had enough prob-lems of his own without having to worry about Ryan. Besides, there was nothing Andy could do about it anyway. Or was there?

Andy chewed on his apple while he thought about Ryan. Maybe he could go back to his desk and pretend to be looking for a book. If Ryan was in the classroom, then Andy could offer to draw pictures with him. He knew Ryan loved to draw pictures of cars and dinosaurs.

But what if Ryan was in the cafeteria chowing down on junk food? Maybe Andy could offer to share his apples and cheese with him. If what Andy's mother said was really true about people stuffing themselves with food when they felt bad, then Ryan might like the cheese and apples almost as much as the candy and pop. Then again, maybe not.

And what if Andy's friends caught him sitting with Ryan? That could spell big trouble. The other kids just didn't like Ryan. And if he started spending any time with Ryan, then Andy might just end up not having any friends either. And that wouldn't help anyone.

The lunch break would be over in another fifteen minutes, so if Andy was going to do something about Ryan today, he'd better do it now.

Should he just forget about Ryan and his problems or try to help?

If you were Andy, and you had to choose, what would *you* do? Why?

More to think about:

Why do you think the kids are teasing Ryan?

Why can't the other kids understand how Ryan feels, the way Andy does?

Why didn't Andy stick up for Ryan when the name-calling started?

Did Ryan do the right thing by walking away?

To Tell or Not to Tell

Jason watched Ms. Thomas write the name of the police officer on the blackboard. He knew what was coming: a talk about shoplifting and how much it cost everyone, not just the stores. It meant higher prices for the shoppers, too.

Jason had heard the same talk last year in the second grade. Only things were different then. He hadn't known any shoplifters.

Now he knew a real shoplifter and he knew him real well. It was his best friend, Dave. At first, Dave said he did it "for kicks," and he had just taken stuff like candy bars and chewing gum.

But now Jason knew that Dave had stolen some golf balls from a sporting goods store and a combination lock from a hardware store. There was probably more stuff, but Jason didn't even want to know about it. He figured what he didn't know couldn't hurt him.

Jason glanced across the room at Dave to see how he was taking the talk. If Jason had been in his place, his face would have been bright red by now and he'd probably be throwing up all over his desk. But Dave was sitting there in his seat—very cool, with a smile on his face. He was actually smiling at the officer.

As Lt. Benjamin finished his talk, he reminded the class that shoplifting was a serious crime and that anyone who didn't report a shoplifter was as guilty as the shoplifter.

Jason scrunched down even lower in his seat and avoided looking at the officer. Instead, he glanced back at Dave who was still smiling, like everything was just great.

That night Jason tossed and turned in his bed. He knew what Dave was doing was wrong, but Dave was his best friend. And you just don't squeal on your best friend.

He had tried telling Dave that shoplifting was wrong, but Dave just laughed at him and told him it was no big deal. He said the stores could afford to lose a few bucks and, besides, he got a "big charge" out of doing it. He didn't plan to stop—ever.

Maybe Jason could talk to his older brother, Eric, about Dave. He could talk to Eric about almost anything, and talking to his brother wouldn't really be the same as "squealing" since Eric was still a kid, too. But what if Eric told one of his buddies and it got spread all over the high school?

There was always Mr. Brown, the school counselor. School counselors were supposed to keep whatever you said to them "confidential" and not tell anyone else. But was telling a school counselor almost like telling the police? What if Mr. Brown told the school principal, Mr. Hanson? And then what if Mr. Hanson told the police? Jason would have to think about this a lot more before he decided to do anything.

Jason knew his dad would be glad to help him. Dad always told him to come to him any time he had a problem. But what if Dad told him to stop seeing Dave? He didn't want to have to give up his best friend. What if Dad didn't understand how important it was to have a best friend?

The more Jason thought about it, the more confused he got. There just didn't seem to be any easy answer to his problem.

If you were Jason, and you had to choose, what would *you* do? Why?

More to think about:

Why do you think Dave shoplifts?

Do you think shoplifting is really a serious crime?

What do you think Jason's brother Eric would tell him to do?

Why do you think the police officer says that not reporting a shoplifter is like doing it yourself?

What might Dave's life be like if he never gets caught shoplifting? What might his life be like if he does get caught?

Tough Call

Mike's baseball team, the Tigers, was ahead by one run in the bottom of the ninth inning. The Wildcats had two outs with one guy on first when their batter hit a ground ball to Mike, who was playing second base. Mike fielded the grounder and tried to tag the runner going from first to second base.

The umpire called the runner out, which meant the game was over and Mike's team had won. But Mike knew that he hadn't actually tagged the runner.

At the last minute, his foot had slipped and his mitt with the ball in it had just barely missed the runner. Even the runner thought he had been tagged because it was such an easy play. Only Mike knew that he had blown it.

Mike started to correct the umpire and tell him that the runner was really safe, but when he opened his mouth, no words came out.

Mike knew that if the umpire changed the call, then the Wildcats would still have a chance to win the game. And if the Wildcats won the game, it would be his fault.

That would make him just about the most unpopular guy on his team for the rest of the season. And what about next year? Would the guys still want him on their team?

Whatever he was going to do, he had to do it fast because his team was already beginning to celebrate their "win."

As he headed back to the dugout, Mike considered telling his teammates the truth, but he knew how important winning was to some of the guys. They would probably just tell him that the umpire's call was final and that, for the good of the team, he should just keep his mouth shut.

Mike knew his teammates well enough to know that some of them would be really angry if he ruined this big opportunity for them.

The Wildcats were the toughest team in the league, and this win could really help the Tigers move up in the rankings.

The Tigers' coach, Mr. Brady, would know what to do, but he was on vacation this week. The dad who was subbing for Mr. Brady was just helping out while Mr. Brady was gone, and Mike didn't really want to put him on the spot with a problem like this.

Just how important was winning? Was it more important than anything else? He knew a lot of the guys thought it was.

If he told the truth, Mike knew he would be in big trouble with some of the other guys. They would probably avoid him for the rest of the season. Or worse. But would his real friends stick by him? He wasn't sure.

Mike's parents had always told him to do what he thought was right regardless of what other people thought or did, but he knew his friends would tell him "not to make waves."

His friends were important to him and he sure didn't want to get a reputation for being the guy who "messed everything up" with his big mouth.

Mike wasn't sure what he should do. He didn't want to make his teammates mad at him, but he didn't think his team should win a game they didn't deserve to win.

What he did know was that he had run out of time. Whatever he was going to do, he had to do it now because both teams were lining up to shake hands.

If you were Mike, and you had to choose, what would *you* do? Why?

More to think about:

Does it really matter *how* you win?

If Mr. Brady, the coach, were there, what do you think he would say?

What do you think the other team would say if they knew what Mike knows?

Would it make Mike's decision easier if the error had been made early in the game rather than at the end?

Trick or Treat

Tonight was supposed to be fun. It was Halloween and Hal was going trick-or-treating with his older brother, Rick. Their costumes had been ready for weeks. Hal had thought about nothing else for days.

Almost nothing else. Unfortunately, Hal found himself in the wrong place at the wrong time earlier in the day. He was in the boys' restroom at noon and he overheard some sixth-graders talking about their plans for Halloween night. Their "fun" included a lot of spray paint, rolls of toilet paper, and lawn bags full of trash. Their target was Mr. Buckingham, a retired school bus driver who lived by himself at the end of Oak Street.

Hal had to admit that Mr. Buckingham wasn't the friendliest guy in the world. He yelled at the kids and chased them with a broom when they tried to steal a few apples from his trees. And he never answered his door on Halloween. But no one deserved to get the treatment Mr. Buckingham was going to get that night.

That afternoon, as Hal pulled on his "Incredible Hulk" costume, he thought about Mr. Buckingham. When he pictured Mr. Buckingham's lawn littered with trash, his garage door spray painted with graffiti, and his trees plastered with toilet paper, Hal's stomach turned flipflops. Somehow Halloween no longer seemed like much fun.

Hal knew he couldn't tell anyone what he knew without getting himself in serious trouble with the sixth-graders, since they would know that he was the one who told. But he wasn't sure he could just stand by and do nothing either.

He thought about telling his brother Rick, but he was a sixth-grader. He would probably just stick up for his friends. He'd probably say that what his friends were going to do to Mr. Buckingham was just a little "harmless fun" and that Mr. Buckingham deserved whatever he got.

There was always Hal's best friend, Bruce. He was in the third grade, too, and he was going to come over and go trick-or-treating with Hal and Rick. He might even be on his way over right now.

Maybe Hal and Bruce could clean up the mess for Mr. Buckingham tomorrow after school, but then would Mr. Buckingham think they were responsible for the mess? He probably would. How could they explain everything without getting the sixth-graders in trouble?

Hal pulled his mask over his head and looked in the mirror. Wow, he even scared himself. What a great costume. Too bad he wasn't really the "Incredible Hulk." Then he could just scare the sixth-graders away from Mr. Buckingham's house.

When his dad got back from a business trip, Hal would have to thank him for the great costume. If his dad were here now, he would know what to do. But he wasn't. He wouldn't be back for two more days and Hal couldn't wait that long. Hal had to figure out what he was going to do *today*.

There was always his mother, but she already had a lot on her mind with her new job and taking care of things while their dad was gone. Besides, he wasn't sure if moms knew much about "guy-type" problems like this.

There was his teacher, Ms. Thomas. He could talk to her at school tomorrow, but she was a girl, too, like his mom. Besides, she taught third grade. Would she know anything about sixth-graders?

Hal wanted to tell someone about his problem, but he didn't know if anyone could really help him. He wanted to do what was right, but he sure didn't want to get himself into trouble.

If you were Hal, and you had to choose, what would *you* do? Why?

More to think about:

Do you think what the sixth-graders plan to do to Mr. Buckingham is just a little "harmless fun"?

How do you think Mr. Buckingham will feel if the sixth-graders do trash his yard? How will he act toward sixth-graders in the future?

If Hal's dad were there, what do you think he would tell Hal to do?

What advice do you think Hal's mom and Ms. Thomas might give him?

103

Tug-of-War

Sarah, Rebekah, and Elizabeth had been best friends since the first grade. Now they were in the fourth grade and they were still best friends. At least they were until two weeks ago.

Sarah and Rebekah had a terrible fight over a part in the class play and they had not spoken to each other for over a week now.

Somehow, Elizabeth had been dragged into the middle of the mess. During gym class, Sarah told Elizabeth that if Elizabeth ever talked to Rebekah again, Sarah wouldn't be her friend. Then Rebekah cornered Elizabeth in the school cafeteria and told her the same thing: that if Elizabeth ever talked to Sarah again, Rebekah wouldn't be her friend.

Elizabeth liked both of her friends and did not want to have to choose between them.

The war between Sarah and Rebekah was really heating up. Sarah told Elizabeth she would take her to the circus if she chose her as her best friend. And Rebekah told Elizabeth that she would take her to the amusement park if she chose her.

Elizabeth thought about asking the school counselor to talk to her friends, but she decided that wasn't a good idea. Sarah and Rebekah would probably tell the counselor to mind her own business and they both would end up mad at Elizabeth for getting the counselor involved.

Elizabeth knew she could try and wait it out and not talk to either friend until they began talking to each other, but that could take a long time. It had been almost two weeks already and there was no sign that things were getting any better.

If anything, things were only getting worse because both of her friends had told Elizabeth that she had to choose between them. And she had to choose *now*. They told her that she could not keep both of them as friends. She had to choose just one. And she had to choose by Friday.

That gave Elizabeth two more days to do something she didn't want to do. She didn't want to have to choose between her two friends. She wanted to keep both of them.

The more she thought about her problem, the angrier she got. Her best friends were trying to make her do something she didn't want to do. Maybe she wouldn't choose either one of them.

Elizabeth thought about talking things over with Ms. Emerson, her favorite teacher, who had known all three girls for more than two years now. She might have some good ideas.

But that would be almost the same as talking to the school counselor.

Elizabeth was sure that neither friend would want her talking about their problem to anyone else, and that included Ms. Emerson.

Elizabeth was left with few choices. She could choose Sarah as her best friend. She could choose Rebekah as her best friend. Or she could refuse to choose either one of them.

If she refused to choose between them, they might just end up getting mad at *her* for not choosing. Sarah and Rebekah could end up best friends with each other again while Elizabeth would end up losing both of them.

If you were Elizabeth, and you had to choose, what would *you* do? Why?

More to think about:

How do you feel about Sarah and Rebekah?

What is a "best friend"?

What do you think Sarah and Rebekah will do if Elizabeth refuses to choose between them? Would it help if Elizabeth could explain to them why she can't decide?

When Is a Promise Not a Promise?

Rachel sat alone in her tree house trying to figure out how she had gotten herself into such a mess. She scraped the last of the peanut butter out of the jar with her finger and then licked it off while she decided what to do.

She loved her older sister, Andrea, but now that Andrea was in junior high, she was becoming impossible. She dressed like her friends, she talked like her friends, and now she was trying to lose weight so she would even look like her friends.

Andrea had found a secret way to keep her weight down, but she had made Rachel promise *never* to tell anyone her secret. Rachel had promised, but now she was sorry she had made the promise.

She knew what Andrea was doing was wrong. And she knew from some of the things she'd seen on TV that what Andrea was doing could hurt her, a lot.

Andrea was proud of what she was doing and thought it was really smart. She bragged to Rachel that she could eat as much as she wanted to and still stay skinny forever. All she had to do was throw up after her biggest meal every day and no one would ever know how she was staying so skinny.

Rachel thought some of Andrea's friends were too skinny, but she never told Andrea that. If her sister wanted to hang out with a bunch of skinny girls, that was her choice.

At first, Rachel had figured that pretty soon her mom or dad would catch on to what Andrea was doing. But no such luck. Andrea ate just like everyone else at the table and then always ran the shower while she was throwing up, so no one would know what she was doing. Their parents just figured Andrea was on a "clean" kick.

Even Rachel didn't know what Andrea really looked like anymore. There was no way to tell what kind of body was hiding there under all the baggy sweatshirts and jeans Andrea wore to school, to soccer practice, and even to her youth group meetings.

Rachel had heard about young girls who ended up in the hospital when they did what Andrea was doing. And she didn't want that to happen to her sister.

Rachel wished now that Andrea had never told her anything. But she had. So now Rachel was stuck with the toughest decision of her life.

What if she said nothing to anyone and something happened to Andrea? Like she ended up passing out in the middle of a busy street? Or what if she ended up in the emergency room of the hospital?

If something bad happened to her sister, then Rachel would be responsible for not getting her the help she needed.

What if Rachel told their parents? They would probably rant and rave for a while, but they would get Andrea the help she needed. But would Andrea ever forgive her for breaking her promise? It would be really awful to have your only sister never speak to you again.

How about telling a school counselor? Ms. Franklin would know what to do in cases like this, and Rachel knew from her friends that she could keep secrets. But would telling a total stranger such a secret be worse than talking to a member of the family?

How about Grandma? Both Andrea and Rachel were close to her. They could tell her anything. And they usually did. But she was getting pretty old. Would she even understand a problem like Andrea's?

Rachel stuck the empty peanut butter jar in her backpack and came down from the tree-house. She still didn't know what she was going to do, but she knew that somehow she had to get her sister the help she needed.

If you were Rachel, and you had to choose, what would *you* do? Why?

More to think about:

Why do you think it's so important to Andrea that she look like her friends?

How serious do you think Andrea's problem really is?

Do you think it's ever okay to break a promise?

What do you think could happen to Andrea if she keeps on eating and throwing up?

Who's to Know?

Wendy and Robin loved karate and they always entered as many local tournaments as they could.

They were both green belts now and would be testing for their purple belts in the spring. They were going to stick with their karate until they earned their black belts. And maybe they would even try for their second-degree black belts.

They had looked forward to this Saturday for more than a month and now, finally, they were at their very first regional tournament. The place was packed. There were white belts, gold belts, green belts, purple belts, blue belts, red belts, brown belts, and black belts all over the place. And there were white uniforms, black uniforms, red uniforms, brown uniforms, blue uniforms, and gray uniforms. Colors they had never seen before. And loads of kids they had never seen before.

They were getting ready to register for their green-belt form class when they saw another kid from their karate school registering at a different table.

Wendy and Robin knew the kid was ten just like them, but he was registering at the table for kids ages eight to nine. If he could do it, why couldn't they?

The competition wouldn't be as stiff in a younger age division and they would have a better chance to win a trophy. Or at least a ribbon.

At a regional tournament there were so many people that no one ever checked the ages of the contestants. And who would care anyway?

Wendy poked Robin in the ribs and told her she was going to register at the other table with the younger kids.

Wendy waited for Robin to join her, but Robin wasn't sure she wanted to. She had never lied about her age before at any of the smaller tournaments and she sure didn't want to start now. But she told herself it really wouldn't be much of a lie because she had just turned ten a month ago. Probably no one except Wendy even knew how old she really was.

Robin watched while Wendy filled out the form for the younger class. What if their karate instructor found out what they had done? He was always talking about how karate builds good character and teaches self-discipline.

Lying about her age to win a ribbon or a trophy wasn't something Robin would be proud of. And what if she did win the trophy? How would she feel every time she looked at it? Would it remind her how she had cheated to get it?

But didn't everyone cheat a little bit to get ahead these days? People lied and cheated all the time. She even knew kids in her own class who cheated on their tests and *they* never got caught. Sometimes you have to cheat just to get something you really wanted: good grades, a good job, or a karate trophy.

How would she feel if Wendy won a ribbon or a trophy and she didn't? They both probably had a good chance of winning ribbons in the younger age division and if Wendy was going to do it, why shouldn't she do it too?

Wendy finished filling out her entry form and then handed Robin another form for the same class. Robin had no more time to make up her mind. She knew she had to decide now.

If you were Robin, and you had to choose, what would *you* do? Why?

More to think about:

What do you think their karate instructor will do if he finds out that Wendy and Robin cheated at the tournament?

Do you think that these days just about everyone cheats to get what they want?

Why do you think people enter these tournaments?

How do you think the younger kids would feel if they knew older kids were entering against them?